Gate Theatre presents

LAND WITHOUT DREAMS / LANDET UDEN DRØMME

Created by Fix&Foxy

Written and directed by Tue Biering

Directed by Lise Lauenblad (London)

Translated from the Danish by Sophie H. Smith

CAST

The Woman   Temi Wilkey

CREATIVE TEAM

Director and Writer	Tue Biering
Director (London)	Lise Lauenblad
Translator	Sophie H. Smith
Sound Designer	Janus Jensen
Assistant Director	Sara Malik
Production Manager	Ed Borgnis
Stage Manager – book	Summer Keeling
Stage Manager – props	Sayeedah Supersad
Intimacy Director	Yarit Dor

CAST

TEMI WILKEY
THE WOMAN

Temi trained at Cambridge University. Her theatre credits include: *Terminal 3 & Act* (Print Room); *Jubilee* (Lyric Hammersmith, Royal Exchange); *The Comedy of Errors* (National Theatre Learning); *How to Hold Your Breath* (The Royal Court); *The World's Wife, Macbeth* and *Private Peaceful* (National Youth Theatre REP Company). Television credits include: *Years and Years* (BBC) and *Manhunt* (ITV). Temi is also a playwright and her debut play, *The High Table* opens at the Bush Theatre in February next year.

CREATIVE TEAM

TUE BIERING
DIRECTOR AND WRITER

Over the last twenty years Tue Biering has initiated and directed a wide range of performances: new dramatic pieces, classics, operas and interactive performances, among others. Biering takes on our notions of the world and shows audiences new aspects of what surrounds us all and of the stories we believed we knew. Under the pseudonym Fix&Foxy, he turns classics into hyperreal performances by staging 'real' people instead of performers.

LISE LAUENBLAD
DIRECTOR (LONDON)

Lise graduated from the Danish Performing Arts School in 2010. She received the Reumert Talent Award in 2012. Her work includes: *Craftsmen* (Royal Theater); *Army*, *Boys Don't Cry / Mungo Park*; *King Arthur* and *This Is Not the Stjernekrigstriologi*. Other credits include: *And Then You Are Suddenly There* (Theater ZeBU); *Peter and the Wolf* (Teater Grob); *The Laugh and the Death (The Floating Theater)*; Afraid of the Dark (ZeBU); *Petra Von Kant* (Aalborg Theater); *A Doll's House* (Fix&Foxy); *The Martyr and the Monk* (The Floating Theater) and *Dancer in the Dark* (Aarhus Theater).

SOPHIE H. SMITH
TRANSLATOR

JANUS JENSEN
SOUND DESIGNER

Janus graduated from the Danish National School of Performing Art in 2001. Janus has collaborated with Fix&Foxy on several projects, including sound designing the original *Land Without Dreams* (Royal Danish Theatre); *Mod Alle Odds* and *S/H* (Frederiksbergscenen NBT). His international touring credits include: *Bosch Dreams* (The 7 Fingers); *The Tiger Lillies Hamlet* and *Det Nye Menneske / The Posthuman*.

SARA MALIK
ASSISTANT DIRECTOR

Sara Aniqah Malik trained as a Director at the Bristol Old Vic Theatre School. As Assistant Director, credits include: *Two Trains Running* (Royal & Derngate & ETT); *Wolfie* (Theatre503); *The Life and Adventures of Nicholas Nickleby* (Bristol Old Vic) and *Mrs Beeton Says* (Redgrave Theatre). As Director, credits include: *Poison* (The Wardrobe Theatre); *Salaam* (VAULT Festival 2019); *The Manual of Little Wars* (RichMix) and *Mary Stuart* (BOVTS Studio).

ED BORGNIS
PRODUCTION MANAGER

Ed is a Production Manager working in the UK and Worldwide. Recent projects include: *Impossible* (a world tour for Jamie Hendry Productions); *Mozart vs. Machine* (Mahogany); *Austentatious* (West End for Underbelly); *Cathy* (Cardboard Citizens); *Disco Pigs* (Tara Finney Productions); *Black and Gold, a Google Christmas Party* (Roundhouse); a series of *Star Wars* launch events (HP) and *The Grand Journey* (European tour for Bombay Sapphire). Ed has worked for the Sound departments of the RSC, Royal Ballet, Regent's Park Open Air Theatre, The Globe, The Tricycle and various concert venues. He also dabbles in video design and provides broadcast engineering support for the BBC. Ed has a Postgraduate Engineering degree from University of Warwick and grew up in London and Norfolk.

SUMMER KEELING
STAGE MANAGER – BOOK

Summer graduated from Mountview Academy of Theatre arts in 2017. Her recent credits include: *A Wake in Progress* (Underbelly Cowgate); *Flinch* (Old Red Lion); *Bromley Bedlam Bethlehem* (Old Red Lion); *Dick Whittington* (Kenton Theatre); *Tour De Ned* (Tour) and *Wind in the Willows* (Tour).

YARIT DOR
INTIMACY DIRECTOR

(ANTI)EST.1979

GATE
theatre

ABOUT THE GATE THEATRE

'London's most relentlessly ambitious theatre'
Time Out

The Gate Theatre was founded in 1979 to present groundbreaking international plays to a London audience.

Today, the Gate exists to make international theatre that asks essential questions about ourselves, each other and the world. Our work investigates what it means to be alive now.

We imagine our work as a live conversation with our audience. Everyone is welcome in our intimate 75 seat theatre. Our space transforms with every production – no two visits are ever the same.

We nurture the best and most diverse new talent to push the boundaries of what theatre is and what else it could be. We create space for radical, inventive thinking to surprise, delight, challenge and inspire.

Our mission and our approach to delivering it strives to embody our organisational values of community, diversity, invention, internationalism and sustainability.

Supported using public funding by
**ARTS COUNCIL
ENGLAND**

(ANTI)EST.1979

GATE
theatre

Each year, the Gate needs to raise over £280,000 in philanthropic support in order to keep taking challenging artistic risks whilst keeping ticket prices low and affordable for all. Our Supporters play a very real and important part in helping us to continue to nurture and support emerging international artists whilst ensuring that their work is made accessible to wide and diverse audiences, and expanding our vital community work.

Our Supporters sit right at the heart of the Gate and are invited behind the scenes to discover more about our productions and meet our exciting artists, the theatre leaders of tomorrow.

Please join and help us continue to grow our activities and support the most exceptional new talent.

To make a gift or join as a Gate Supporter, please contact

development@gatetheatre.co.uk

020 7229 5387

www.gatetheatre.co.uk

Land Without Dreams is kindly supported by the Embassy of Denmark London.

The Gate Theatre's 40th anniversary season is supported by Cockayne – Grants for the Arts and the London Community Foundation.

COCKAYNE   The London Community Foundation

We are grateful to the following individuals and Trusts and Foundations for their support of the Gate's work.

SPECIAL THANKS TO
David and Jean Grier and Addy Loudiadis.

GATE PIONEERS AND GUARDIANS
Kate Maltby, Charles and Barbara Prideaux, Linda and David Lakhdhir.

GATE AMBASSADORS
Eva Boenders and Scott Stevens, David Lacey, Kirsty and Iona Luke, David and Susie Sainsbury, Jon and NoraLee Sedmak and Sandi and Jake Ulrich.

GATE KEEPERS
The Agency (London) Ltd., Bruno and Christiane Boesch, Ariane Braillard and Francesco Cincotta, Dr Geraldine Brodie, Sarah and Phillippe Chappatte, Charles Cormick, Robert Devereux, Charles Glanville and James Hogan, Richard and Jan Grandison, Anatol Orient and Stephanie and Aaron Pottruck Goldman.

Thank you to all our Gate Openers and other supporters, and those who wish to remain anonymous.

TRUSTS AND FOUNDATIONS
Arts Council England, Jerwood Arts, Backstage Trust, the Royal Borough of Kensington and Chelsea, the Goethe-Institut, Cockayne – Grants for the Arts, the London Community Foundation and Ernest Hecht Charitable Foundation and National Lottery Awards for All.

CORPORATE SUPPORTERS
Douglas & Gordon

JERWOOD DESIGNERS AT THE GATE

Since 2001, the Jerwood Designers Programme has given outstanding designers and design assistants in the early stages of their careers the unique opportunity to design a full production at the Gate Theatre whilst developing their experience and expertise.

This partnership is an essential part of the Gate's identity as a theatre – enabling us to offer designers the opportunity to completely re-imagine how our space is configured for every show. Alumni of the programme include Chloe Lamford, Jon Bausor, Fly Davis, Soutra Gilmour, Tom Scutt and Rosie Elnile.

'Ground-breaking and visionary design is a key part of the Gate Theatre's identity. This reputation has been built on the generous support of Jerwood Arts and we are hugely grateful for it.'

Ellen McDougall, Artistic Director

Jerwood Arts is the leading independent funder dedicated to supporting UK artists, curators and producers to develop and thrive. We enable transformative opportunities for individuals across art forms, supporting imaginative awards, bursaries, fellowships, projects, programmes and commissions. We present new work and bring people from across the arts together through our exhibitions and events in London, as well as across the UK. www.jerwoodarts.org

GREEN GATE

We want to imagine a different, better future with everyone who comes through our doors.

At the Gate Theatre, we recognise that we have a vital part to play in changing attitudes and approaches to environmental sustainability and climate justice. We tell stories that help us question and imagine who we are as individuals and as communities, our social responsibility, and our future. We are passionate about ensuring that our programming is underpinned by recognition of this responsibility.

The Gate was founded in 1979 to present ground-breaking international work, and so the narrative around climate justice is intrinsic to the work we make and how we run our organisation: global equality, conflict and the natural world are inextricably linked, and an essential component of a theatre with an international outlook.

'The climate crisis is also a crisis of the imagination. If we cannot imagine a more sustainable and just way of living we cannot achieve it. Artistic and cultural institutions can be powerhouses of change, helping to create and forge new ways of thinking and doing. Now is the time to meet the emergency with imagination.'

Anthony Simpson-Pike, Associate Artist

We are very happy to report that we have been awarded 4 stars from Julie's Bicycle Creative Green Assessment for our actions and efforts in making sustainable theatre.

Creative Green is a certification from Julie's Bicycle which provides organisations with a systematic, achievable and inspiring approach to environmental sustainability. It celebrates environmental success and shines a light on areas for improvement and gives your organisation a star rating from 1 to 5.

A MANIFESTO FOR OUR FUTURE

PROCESS IS POLITICAL

It is relevant who makes the work.
Amplify the voices silenced by the canon.
Text is not the only form of authorship.
Our artists are international.
Our shows are multilingual.
Our rehearsals are open.

FORM IS POLITICAL

Look outside what you know.
Rethink definitions of excellence.
Celebrate subjectivity.
Celebrate the mess and imperfection of humanity.
Celebrate liveness.

OUR WORK IS PART OF THE WORLD

Acknowledge and hold the suffering of the past.
Imagine the future.
Don't portray the world, change it.
We are nature and nature is us.
There must be space to come together and talk.
We declare a climate emergency.

CHANGE. TRANSITION. TRANSFORM.

Make work in a circular economy (and only 20% of materials can be new).
The shows (and all the conversations too) must leave the building.
Texts from earlier than 2010 must be radically interrogated.
At least one show in every season must be made outside the UK.
Everyone in the room is part of the show (this includes the audience).
We can't do this without you.
What happens after the play is the point of the play.

LAND WITHOUT DREAMS
(LANDET UDEN DRØMME)

Tue Biering

LAND WITHOUT DREAMS

Landet Uden Drømme

Translated from the Danish by Sophia H. Smith

OBERON BOOKS
LONDON

WWW.OBERONBOOKS.COM

First published in 2019 by Oberon Books Ltd
521 Caledonian Road, London N7 9RH
Tel: +44 (0) 20 7607 3637 / Fax: +44 (0) 20 7607 3629
e-mail: info@oberonbooks.com
www.oberonbooks.com

A catalogue record for this book is available from the British Library.

PB ISBN: 9781786829061
E ISBN: 9781786829054

Cover image: Rosie Elnile / Emma Digby

Printed and bound by 4EDGE Limited, Hockley, Essex, UK.
eBook conversion by Lapiz Digital Services, India.

10 9 8 7 6 5 4 3 2 1

PART ONE

(There's full light on the empty stage and on the seats when the audience enters. The light is kept that way without any change for most of the performance.)

1.

IN THE NEAR PAST

(A woman walks on stage.)

Now imagine that it's completely dark.
You can't see anything.
There are no sounds.

Then, a light turns on.
Imagine a room.
It looks like this one,
but there's nobody on stage.
Nobody in the seats. It's completely empty.
Nothing is happening.
Time passes.

Then the door opens.
The audience comes in.
They look like you.
They talk to each other.

Some of them are talking about how long it's been since they've seen something really good in the theatre.

Two of them are talking about where they're going for the summer holidays.

There is a couple, who are on their first date. You sit down at the very back, but you don't yet know whether you'll be sitting close together and holding hands or whether you should start off by resting your hands in your laps. You decide to leave your hands alone.

One of you is wondering if the title of the play that you're watching right now has something to do with insomnia or maybe it's more of a metaphor.

Another person in here loves sci-fi. You love sci-fi because anything can happen. Nothing can be called unrealistic because it's about the future, and no one knows what that'll bring. You're really excited to see how they'll do sci-fi in the theatre.

THE PLAY BEGINS

The lights on the audience are switched off and the lights on the stage fade up. There is still nothing in the room.

One person is thinking:
"Is that really it? Where's the set? Where's the scenography?"

You, who'd been so looking forward to seeing some sci-fi, can feel the disappointment spreading itself.
"Where's the room that's supposed to look like something from the future?"

There's a long pause.
Nothing happens.

Someone lets their eyes wander.

(The description of the room ends at the door.)

Right behind the door stands a woman.
She's biting her bottom lip.
In just a few moments, she'll meet about (the number of audience members that evening) people.
They don't know this, but she knows all of them.

6

She has to tell them something they'll have a hard time believing. It will be intense and change their lives, but she's heard that people who go to the theatre are always very open-minded. They want to believe everything.
She opens the door.
And enters.

A WOMAN ENTERS

She walks across the stage and stands near its centre.
She is (description of the actress: height and length/colour of hair).
She looks trustworthy, reliable.
She looks out at the audience.
And you look back at her.
Some of you think that it's off to a good start.
(Smiles at some of them.)
Others sit and smile back out of politeness.
(Looking at someone in particular.)
One of you can feel that your underpants have ridden up a bit and you're contemplating how to pull them back down again without anyone noticing.

(Looking at someone specific.)
One of you is wondering if the new season of *The End of the Fucking World* is on Channel 4 yet? Or if that is next Wednesday. And when you can just binge it on Netflix.

One of you is waiting on an important call and your phone is on 'vibrate' – even though you were all told to switch off your cell phones. About once a minute, you place your hand on your pocket, to check if it's vibrating. And if it vibrates, you plan on answering, and leaving, even though you'll have to walk past ten audience members and the woman on stage will notice.

The woman looks at everyone in the room and then she says something that will change everything for all of you.

(Exit.)

2.

THE WOMAN IS FROM THE FUTURE

(Time passes.)
(Enter.)

I come from the future.
Don't be afraid.
All will be well.

I know that a lot of you are worried about what will happen in the future.
Crises, catastrophes, and even more complex issues weigh on your minds and when you look to the future, it only gets worse and worse.

Several of you can't even imagine it being any different.
You've stopped dreaming because it's pointless. Naïve.

I've come from the future to tell you that it's going to be okay.

(Looking at someone in particular.)

Now, you're thinking:
I need some sort of set design to be able to imagine where I'm meant to be. When she says that she's from the future, there could at least be some white glass walls and some sharp white LED lights. Or she could wear sci-fi clothes. Like a tight, sexy, sci-fi outfit.

You, the one on the date, you're thinking about sex with your date. How will it be? Will you already have sex tonight? You definitely want to. Should you take the initiative or let your date make the first move?

Someone in the audience hasn't really been paying attention. You've been sitting and thinking about the conversation that you and your partner have been putting off for years. About getting your eggs and his sperm frozen. You know, just in case. You're thinking that when the show is over, you'll go straight home and talk about it. 'Cause the way things are looking now, it'll only get worse.

The woman on stage can tell that no one is taking her seriously. No one really believes that she's from the future. Everyone thinks that this is theatre. That she's playing a part. That she's just saying some lines.
Some think they've actually seen her in some other play.
Most are impressed that actors can remember so many lines.

(Exit.)

3.

I LOOK LIKE YOU

(Enter.)

I come from the future.
I know I don't look like someone from the future.
I look like you. And that's the point.
I can't look like someone from the future. That would just scare you.
In the future, we don't look like this.
But right now, I look like, what you call, a woman.

I'm wearing clothes that look like yours.
I'm speaking your language, so that you can understand me.
I sit like you. I do this with my hands like you.
(Sits as one of the audience, acts like another, etc.)
I do it so that you can see yourselves in me, recognise yourselves, so that you can feel safe.

With this, I say: I come in peace, do not be afraid.

9

YOU ARE AFRAID

The audience IS afraid.
Only (five percent of the evening's audience) of those who are
sitting in the theatre and looking at the woman who's standing
right here believe that things will get better in the future.
The rest think that the future looks bleak.

They've seen the headlines, watched the documentary, heard it
on the radio, read the book. They see the poles melting, the polar
bears starving. Ecosystems collapsing. Species going extinct.
Others see overpopulation.
Growing inequality.
Increasing political polarisation.
Kids soon losing contact with themselves or with reality.
Technologies taking on human attributes. And soon, humans
are no longer able to compete with artificial intelligence that
possesses emotions and an inexhaustible supply of skills.

All the films with people in tight sci-fi clothes are dystopian
stories about humanity fleeing from a broken, bashed-up,
uninhabitable planet.

The woman on stage, who says she's from the future, smiles,
but she's serious. She tries to speak in calm, convincing tones.
I understand that some of you are afraid.
The world is changing so quickly, you're having a hard time
keeping up.
You're used to being able to take action, but now many of
you feel as though you have no influence. Everything is
spiralling out of control, and will continue to do so, at a steadily
increasing pace, which you cannot cope or come to terms with.
Imagine that it starts to rain in here.
It begins with one drop.

Now something strange happens in the play.

The moment she says the words, a drop falls from the ceiling. It falls right next to the woman.

You just manage to have the thought that it was a funny coincidence, but you don't have time to think any more before two more drops fall, not far from where the first one fell.

A second later, four drops fall. A second after that, eight.

You can no longer count the drops, but for every second, the number of drops doubles.

Sixteen drops,

thirty-two drops,

sixty-four drops,

one hundred and twenty-eight drops.

And so, it continues.

First you think that it's a special effect. It's pretty impressive. One of you thinks that it is a visual disturbance, like when you have migraines.

It's now constantly raining on stage. And soon the floor is covered in a thin layer of water.

Those of you sitting on the front row lift your feet up a bit. The number of raindrops doubles with each passing second and the water is now rising very quickly. Then it starts to rain above the audience. And it becomes heavier and heavier. Everyone is wet. The water reaches two meters. And those who were sitting in the front rows are now lying flat and trying to keep themselves afloat.

Two seconds later, the water has reached the ceiling. And after a few minutes, everyone in here has drowned. Your bodies are now lying up against the ceiling, your lungs are filled with water.

None of you managed to grow gills.

There wasn't enough time.

And then, with a blink of an eye, you're back in the room. For one short moment, you weren't here.

It felt real. But your clothes are dry and nothing is dripping from the ceiling. You're sitting in your seats and you're looking at the woman who's talking to you.

The woman says:
Technological development is at the point where the water just about covers the floor.
But you've got a strong feeling that this is only the beginning.
Disaster seems impossible to prevent.
The future is lost on the floor.

Well, there went that date, the two of you on the date think.
It would've been better with a trip to the cinema.

The two of you, who'd talked about where you were going for the summer holidays when you first entered the theatre, are now considering staying home and taking a camping trip instead.

(Exit.)

4.

YOU ARE THE CHOSEN ONES

(Entrance.)

There is a reason why precisely all of you are here tonight.
You're going to make a difference.
You've all got many different reasons for being here, but it's not a coincidence that you're sitting here together.

You are important for the future.
If you really think about it, you've always felt this.
That you've been chosen.
That you were created for a precise purpose.
That you were going to accomplish something special.
It is a feeling that was strongest in you as a child.
But you waited for too long, waited for the secret sign or signal. It never came.

And later on, you forgot the feeling. And maybe it's been a long time since you last felt it.

Right now, you're maybe not feeling so chosen. But you are! You are important to the future I come from.

(Looking at someone specific.)

One of you, in here, right now, feels seen by the woman on stage. That's exactly the feeling you felt as a child. That's why you went into politics. Even though, lately, you've had a hard time restoring the belief that you're actually making a difference. Politics is difficult, and you feel as though your voters don't get this, when they think that just about anything is possible with a snap of the fingers. You can't just sit and wait for a miracle to happen tomorrow. You must take concrete political steps today, even though it's far from the path you thought you'd take.

You, who's sitting somewhere in here, with your phone on vibrate, are still waiting for the call. It's a phone call from the company that made a hiring profile on you. Tonight is the night you find out whether you get the job. You hope the woman on stage is right. That you are the chosen one.

THE AUDIENCE WANTS CATASTROPHE

Right now, a sense of unease is spreading through some of you in the audience. When is the play actually starting? When will something dramatic happen?

Where is the crisis? The catastrophe?

You're used to that being what it's all about.

That someone dies. Or an epidemic breaks out.

Soon, she'll be shot. Or she'll find out that she's got cancer.

Soon, the world will end. You can feel it in your body. Your body is tense and ready.

But nothing happens.

She leaves.

INTERMEZZO

(Scratching her skin. Rubbing her body up against the wall.)

5.

THE FUTURE

The door opens and the woman walks in again. She says:

In the future, a word like 'catastrophe' doesn't exist
Nor will the word 'dystopia'
Or the word 'worry'
Or 'politically correct.'
One does not say: 'it's an uphill battle'
Or 'the glass is half empty'
The word 'anxiety' does not exist
Crisis
Problem
Or the word 'challenge,' when it is used to mean crisis or problem
The end of the world
Climate crisis
Financial crisis
Mid-life crisis
Humanitarian crisis
Refugee crisis
Personal crisis
Identity crisis
Relationship crisis
Audience crisis
Job crisis
Solidarity crisis
Sex crisis

(Looking at someone in particular.)

One of you, in the audience, is squirming in your chair, you can't help it, it's so painfully awkward to listen to some stupid actor use up all her stage time to paint such a pathetically positive picture of the future.

You believe that positive thinking is decidedly dumb and counterproductive. You've always done best with challenge and adversity.

(Pause.)

The rest of you, most of you, aren't taking what the woman is saying seriously. It's just theatre. And you're used to hearing that one should dream and believe in the best in people. And that's awesome! It makes for a nice and warm feeling on the inside. It's almost like you yourself get good at dreaming, and you get filled with a sense of connection, as though together, humanity can accomplish something great and fantastic. But you also know that this feeling, one moment later, is gone. And then reality comes crashing over you. And that's not something you can dream away.

(Exit.)

6.

THE WOMAN SHOUTS AT THE AUDIENCE

(Enter.)

The woman from the future stands up on a box. Instinctively. For a moment, she doesn't know what she should do up there. But then she takes a deep breath and shouts.
She shouts: "THE FUTURE IS GOOD. YOU HAVE TO BELIEVE IN IT!!!! The future I come from depends on this."

Now the audience starts to realise that she actually means what she's saying. That the woman on stage wants everyone to believe that she's REALLY from the future and that they REALLY have to believe that it'll get better.
Very few people in the audience appreciate being told what they should do, think or believe in.
You are well-read, well-informed independent individuals, who generally are quite tired of people who stand up on boxes and shout.

One of you is thinking: "This is why I never go to the theatre. They shout too much, and you never really fall for what they're saying."

THE OLD LADY

But then something that rarely happens in theatre happens.
One person stands up.
An older woman.
She is angry. And she doesn't care if it's completely inappropriate to talk during a performance.
She yells down to the woman on stage.
"I've heard this bullshit before. That everything is going to be better. That we should look forward. But then what happened!?!?!?!?! Even more bullshit! This was the time that would end all wars. More equality. Free love. Eternal youth. BULLSHIT! BULLSHIT! BULLSHIT!"

The older woman can't contain herself. She walks down towards the woman on the stage. She has tears in her eyes.
She spits, her body is shaking with rage.
"I can't see things getting any damn better. Can anyone see things getting better???"
She looks at the others, sitting in the audience.
"I would rather die today than in ten years!"
She turns on her heel and purposely walks towards the exit, slamming the door on her way out.

Now a young man stands up. He also shouts at the woman on stage. He shouts: "What do you actually want? If you really wanna try convincing us of something, then put on a proper costume!!!"

Several others also consider walking out, but stay seated, because they can't be bothered to face the attention they'd get if they walked out. And the woman would probably comment on it. You decide that, at the very least, you want your money back, and you hope that's possible even though you don't have the reusable ticket because of the recycling policy in this theatre. Hopefully you still have the email confirmation.

The woman on stage looks out at them. She realises that it was a really bad idea to come here. To think that they would listen to her, understand her. She had a feeling that precisely these people, sitting right in front of her, would've been ready.

If only there was one, just one, that believed her, then that would be enough.
But maybe that was naïve.

The woman leaves the stage.

(The light fades down on the stage, leaves it dark.)

7.

THE GIRL IN THE DARK

(The woman enters the audience light.)

The woman has left the stage, like so many times before, but she doesn't come back.
A long time passes.
For some reason, everyone stays seated.
Even those who are looking for their ticket, hoping for a refund.
Maybe because that's what you do in the theatre.

Maybe because they don't know what else to do.

There is one person in the audience, who hopes that the woman will return.
It is a young girl who, throughout the whole play, has hidden in the shadows.
From the moment she saw the woman walk on to the stage for the first time, it was like she was seeing herself.
And when she heard the woman begin to speak, it was like she was hearing her own voice.
It was like the woman was speaking only to her. And when the woman said, "Don't be afraid," it was her the woman was trying to soothe. And when the woman said that it wasn't a coincidence that the audience was here, that they were specially chosen, then the girl knew that it was her, that the woman was referring to. Now she's sitting, hidden in the dark, with the ticket in her hand. She received it by post. There was no sender or return address, but you came here. And you know that this must mean something.
You've been struck by a deep and heavy sadness for a long time. An abysmal darkness that has pulled you down and out of this world.
The woman on stage could see it. And now you're sitting and hoping that the woman will come back. You want to believe. You want to dream. You want to imagine worlds that don't yet exist.

YOU HAVE TO IMAGINE THAT –

(Lights up on stage.)
(The woman returns to centre stage.)

The woman comes back in. She says:

That which sets you apart as humans is your ability to imagine things that aren't in front of you. This has assured your continued survival and helped you evolve into the people you are today.

18

You need to imagine that which you cannot imagine.

You need to imagine a country without central governance.
A country where EVERYONE is part of the same mental network.
A country where people throw a party once in a while just to get to know each other better.
A country where there is no democracy, but rituals, dialogue, and temples.

(Pause.)

A WORLD ONLY OF ANIMALS

And now imagine something else.
Imagine that you're disappearing.
(Pause.)
Of all the animal species on Earth, it is humans that go extinct.
The earth is no longer being cultivated.
Pigs, hens, cows, minks, and…ostriches…many other species must now live without humans.
There will no longer be humans, who can eat and drink and buy things in plastic packaging.
And that is good. No one misses humanity.

INTERMEZZO – JET LAG

(Scratching her skin again. Some skin fall of. Rubbing her body up against the floor, the wall. Moment of tiredness.)

POLITICS IN THE FUTURE

Imagine a world without countries, where there's a group of people sitting together, who are good at talking to each other. They always manage to make one plus one equal five.

They disagree, but they disagree in a good way. And they
all agree that everyone should be happy. Being naïve is cool.
Everyone is naïve. Naiveté is a positive word.
They are good at creating perfect places for people with very
different interests.
And the leader steps down, when there is no more creative or
positive energy left.
Then the leader says, "Let someone else take my place,
someone with the clarity of vision and the energy necessary to
unite and lead," and this doesn't mean blindly uniting behind
the leader or having the exact same ideology or thought.
The unifying force is precisely that there is room for everything.

THE MAN WITH THE TELEPHONE

A phone vibrates. You, who's sitting and waiting for a call
from a recruitment agency, pick up your phone. You don't
recognise the number. It must be the company calling you
directly. You stand up and take the call while passing by the
ten audience members sitting in the row.
Some of you think it's incredibly rude. It rips you out of the
illusion. You get distracted.

The man with the telephone has now left the room. It's not
the company that has called, but the hospital. They tell him
that his daughter has been admitted. She was run down by
a lorry on her way home from a friend's. The man walks
through the foyer, towards the parking lot, where his car is
parked. He is now sitting in his car, on his way out to
(the name of the hospital closest to the evening's venue).
He swerves past a red light on (name of a street near the
venue). And is not sure if he should have driven up (another
street name nearby) instead. Out of the blue, he thinks: "I
forgot my jacket at the theatre."

The audience inside the theatre doesn't know what happened. One of you saw the look in his eye. He looked scared. He seemed worried.

Another person in the audience sat, earlier that day, outside of <u>(the name of the hospital closest to the evening's venue)</u>, where you'd been examined for cervical cancer. You fear that the cell changes you were diagnosed with mean that you have cancer and have to start treatment. You're constantly thinking about it. That you'll miss the chance to have children. About how your life will change.
Four hours ago, you questioned whether you should go to the theatre, but decided that it was easier to do as planned.
You look at the woman who's standing on stage and hope that she can get you to think about something else.

There are still diseases in the future. But it's not dangerous to get sick. The diseases you know of today are curable in the future.
No one dies of diseases.
When someone dies, it's their own choice, because they want to make room for another life.

In the future, there are no white glass walls with inbuilt LED lights. Instead, rooms are so green and so lush that it almost hurts your eyes and makes your mouth water.

In the future, people start believing in the future.
In the future, technology solves many of our problems and gives us the opportunity to spend more time together.
And you don't have to be afraid of being abandoned because there is always someone to be with.
In the future, everyone is equal, and those who like to be unequal, also get to be just that.
And those who want to be humiliated, also get to be humiliated.
In the future, there is no 'wing' politics. Talk of sides, colours, left-wing, right-wing ended a long time ago.

In the future, there is no poverty and there is no famine.
In the future, you don't have to ask yourself whether something
is healthy. It just is.
In the future, you dance like this:
(She dances.)

In the audience, there are now a few people who're starting to smile.
They like the thought of people dancing in the future.
It reminds them of how they dance now.

One person in the audience is thinking that the woman on stage
actually looks pretty cute. It may be that it's all a bit silly, all this
stuff about her coming from the future. About
not being afraid. But she looks cute... And she seems genuine.

IMAGINE A THEATRE AUDIENCE

(A step closer to the audience.)

Imagine
A world
Like this one.
Similar in many ways.
There could be a theatre like this one.
And there could be people, like some of you folks here in the
theatre.
But when you get closer, you can see the difference.
In this world, they smile a bit more.
Not to be polite.
But because they are happy.
They are not afraid – or, they can be afraid – but they are not
afraid of tomorrow or the future. They know that there are still
many things that could be better, but they're convinced that
they'll get better.
Not straight away.
It happens slowly, almost imperceptibly, but they can see it if
they stand still long enough.

Now something strange happens. A small but intense happiness starts to spread through the audience. It feels like a tickle. The kind of tickle you got from your first kiss. Or the first time you felt that there was some sort of connection in life that was greater than yourself. The kind of feeling you can get when you look up at a sky dizzy with stars. There is a feeling, that comes unexpectedly, that is unexplainable. Maybe it is something she said. It's as though a few things are falling into place.

(Exit.)

SHE IS FROM THE FUTURE

(Enter.)

In the play that you're currently watching, you've seen the woman on stage leave the room and come back again. And each time she enters, it's like something has changed. Like something has happened, like time has passed. Isn't her hair a bit longer? Wasn't she wearing different shoes?

Then there's a moment – and that moment is right about now in the play – when someone in the audience gets the thought that it's like there's a time jump every time she leaves the room. She has been somewhere else. This thought leads to the next: It is possible that she's from the future.

The thought is not that foreign to you either. Throughout your life, you have considered the possibility that time travel was possible. And maybe some of you have imagined that, one day, you would meet someone from the future.

Slowly the audience realises that she REALLY is from the future. That EVERYTHING she has said up until now is true.

One of you, who had a hard time with the play in the beginning, now regrets not listening more closely to start off with. You're annoyed at yourself. You may have missed out on something because you were busy doubting it. You think, "Doubt has always been one of my personal strengths. But right now, I do not doubt. She is from the future."

THE MIRACLE

The whole audience starts to listen to her.
She says that she has met you before. Throughout time. Time that you've not yet experienced.

You believe her descriptions of the future. You start imagining new worlds. Nothing can stop you now.

Many have a deep longing to hear something other than doomsday prophecies. They want to give in, dream out loud about something better, without feeling guilty. They want to rekindle the belief that the world can look different. They want to dare to be naïve and to speak out against those who laugh at them.

(Pause.)

At a certain point, the woman on stage stops speaking.

She looks at them. And smiles. Because she can see, that now, they are where they are meant to be. They are ready.

(She walks very slowly towards them.)

THE CONFESSION – GOOD ISN'T WHAT YOU THINK IT IS

I have a confession.
It's not going to be the way I told you it would be.
I've told you a few things that you wanted to hear.
And that's crucial, in order for things to become better.
You need to trust this.
But good is not what you think it is.

If I told you how things really will be, you'd get scared. It's not something you've ever seen before.
It's so different that you can't even imagine it.
It's difficult to explain.
But you shouldn't be afraid. The woman turns around and walks away. The audience knows that she's not coming back. They can feel it.

(Slowly, more light on audience.)

AFTER THE PLAY

Their first impulse is to clap. Because that's what you usually do. But this wasn't a play.
It was something very special.

So instead, they stand up and start to gather their belongings. In complete silence. They don't say anything. They just smile at each other. They feel connected. Chosen.

They leave the room with a feeling that something has changed. They can't put their finger on exactly what has changed, but they can feel it.

The girl, who sat in the dark and saw herself in the woman on stage, goes home and writes a letter to herself. In the letter, she writes: "Don't be afraid." It helps her.

You, who wanted to speak to your partner about freezing your eggs and his sperm, go home and you talk to each other. About your lives. About the world. About how things will work out. About wanting to learn how to sail. Because maybe, one day, people will have to sail to work. It could be fun.

The two of you on a date go home together. You go home and have sex. Fantastic sex. Something that you'll look back on for the rest of your lives as something completely mind-blowing.

You, who loves sci-fi, will take down all of your books and films and posters that depict a dark dystopian future and drop them off at a recycling centre tomorrow. You buy a book about wild flowers and, a few months from now, you'll take over a plot of grass in a public park, where you'll grow wild roses. Later on, they're discovered by the park patrol officer, but they're not removed. On the contrary, a bigger plot is then dedicated to wild plants. And after that, you get hired to transform all parks into wild areas, where animal life can evolve into new species that thrive in cities.

The man whose phone vibrated during the play sits in the hospital for three days, where his daughter is receiving care. On the third day, she dies from internal bleeding and injuries received from a twenty-six-tonne lorry failing to see her turn right. For several months, he feels like he can't move. He quietly waits for a reason to get up. To say something. He starts praying to God. For the first time, and it's not to any god in particular. He prays to God for a time machine. He'll use it to go back to the night he went to the theatre, but instead of going to see the play, he would pick up his daughter, so that she wouldn't have to go home alone. But there is no time machine; it hasn't been invented yet. And he'll never be able to go back and save his daughter. But eventually, he'll think the very thoughts that one day will contribute to making time travel possible.

Forty-seven days after the play, you, who were on your first date, break up. But you remain friends, because today in the theatre you experienced something truly unique.

In two months, one of you will go out dancing and you'll not want to stop. After that, you'll start dancing more in general, in short bursts, you bring dancing into small parts of your life and you feel that it does something good.

(Looking at someone specific.)

In two months, you'll cancel your HBO subscription and start playing the violin. In spite of your advanced age and the demanding nature of the instrument, you become a great talent. You don't perform any concerts or release any of your pieces, but you play for your friends and leave your music on old answering machines around the world.

(Pointing.)
In five months, you'll invest all your money into a company that synthesises poison from frogs. This poison will be used in the treatment for cervical cancer and will contribute towards a cure.

Half a year later, three of you will read at least two of the books that you told others that you had read, even though you hadn't read them yet.

In two years, one of you will develop a vaccine to be developed that mutates uncontrollably and ends in the destruction of a large herd of water buffalo in South East Asia. A consequence of this is the survival of an endangered species of amphibian, which later inspires the development of a biotechnology that allows humans to breathe underwater.

(Looking at someone specific.)
In four years, you'll invent a cosmetic product that'll make everyone more beautiful without actually making any visible changes.

In five years, one of you will break free from your political party, and instead spearhead a project for change. You will let fear be replaced by hope for a better society. You believe that hope is an underlying driving force in all human beings, and you will inspire people to think in new and independent ways. You will revive the dream you had when you were a child.

In fourteen years and three months, one of you will remove all the hair from your body and donate it to others who are more in need of it.

In exactly seventeen years, one of you will die –

in exactly seventeen years and three weeks, three of you will die.

In twenty-two years, you will visit a museum for electrical cords because almost everything will be wireless.

In forty-seven and a half years, three of you will sail to work.

In forty-nine years, you will wear tape instead of underwear. That way, you'll be free of wedgies. In fifty-six years, one of you won't be able to feel anything unless your skin is cut into.

In one hundred and four years, everyone in here will be dead.

(Light fades down on audience, leaves them in the dark.)

Most of you will not have made a great difference. And that's good! It's all part of what contributes towards nature unfolding in the right direction.

(Leaves.)

(She enters with an answering machine, turns it on, places it on the floor. Violin music.)

THE WOMAN WHO DREAMT ABOUT TIME

The woman once dreamt that time moved through her, without her getting any older. Time became a long series of events that she bore witness to and that continued into infinity without ever changing her. In the end, she no longer knew how old she was or which time she was in. Or if there even was such a thing as time. But, in any case, she had been there for a long while, and the world had become another.

(Walks out.)

PART TWO

IMAGINE A BEING

(Enters with a bucket of clay. Dress off. Naked.)

(Stand. Violin music stops.)

Imagine a woman.
She looks a bit like me.
Imagine a woman.
She looks nothing like me.
Imagine a human being, looking neither like a woman or a man.
Imagine a being that doesn't look like anything you've ever
seen before. Imagine that it's intelligent. And that it talks to
you, but you don't understand what it's saying.
But it says:
Imagine a woman.

*(On her knees. She puts clay on her face. In her hair. Makes a creature
with her hair. Clay on her body. All her body covered in white soft clay.)*

WE ARE ALL ALIKE

(She removes the clay from her eyes and looks at the audience.)

We are all alike. Our skin is in the exact same nuances.
There is no difference between us.
Everyone speaks the same language.
Everyone understands each other.

(Exit.)

*(Goes out in a different way. Falls on her way out several times as if
she has become older. Crawls out tired.)*

(Crawls in with a bucket of a slimy substance. Pours the slime over her head. Crawls carefully into the slime cocoon. She moves. Stretches.)

THE JOURNEY

(She lays down in the slime. Completely still.)
(She lies there for a little while.)
(Fetus sleeping movements. Moves toes a bit. Moves fingers a bit.)

1000 YEARS LATER

(The light fades up and down.)
(She starts to spasm.)
(She emerges from the slime.)

SOMETIME IN THE FUTURE, THE JOURNEY BACK

(She speaks, but her voice has changed.)

Imagine…that you can imagine…a future.
Imagine…a future that is good.
In the future, there will be no traffic accidents.
There will be no lorries that blindly turn and kill nine-year-old girls at a green light. In the future, nine-year-old girls that get run over, do not die.
They do not die. Nine-year-old girls cannot die.

In the future, we will invent a little box that can send impulses to a screen, upon which you can see a ball moving from one side to the other, and this way, you can play against each other.

In the future, man will be able to walk on the moon.

We will be able to send messages and news across the world through electric waves.

In the future, we will figure out how to cure diseases with small swallowable white pills.

One day, man will invent a material that is flexible and can be moulded into anything in all sorts of colours.
One day, much later, this material will form large islands that drift the oceans of the world.

In the future, you'll have a glass screen that displays lots of dots of light that together form images of people, animals and things.

In the future, women will be able to vote like men.

Far into the future, humans will fly.

In the future, people will be able to talk to each other across long distances.

In the future, a machine will be invented that is so small it can be placed on a horse-drawn carriage and, with the aid of steam, it will be able to propel the wheels forward, so that the carriage can drive by itself, without horses.

In the future, humans discover a substance, which will end world hunger.

In the future, you'll know why people die when they've cut themselves and fluid comes out of the wound.

In the future, humans will invent a device made of polished pieces of broken glass that will allow you to see what cannot be seen.

In the future, we will find a way to tan the skins of animals and use their intestines, so that we can make shoes and clothes.

In the future, we can sail on the water.

(She starts to stand up.)

31

In the future, you'll begin to imagine things that are not yet there. And you'll paint pictures of it.

In the future, something will be invented that allows human to make fire themselves.
In the future, we will stand up and start walking on two legs.

In the future, we will develop lungs and move up onto land.
In the future, we will split up and become multicellular organisms.

(She leaves.)

THE END

(Light up on the audience. One person in the audience stands up and enters the stage, facing the rest of the audience.)

AUDIENCE 1:
I am from the future.

(Then another one stands up and enters the stage. This time a woman.)

AUDIENCE 2:
I am from the future.

(Five-seven more stand up and go to the stage. They all say:)

AUDIENCE:
I am from the future.

THE LAST AUDIENCE MEMBERS ON STAGE:
I am from the future. Do not be afraid.

(Blackout.)

WWW.OBERONBOOKS.COM